THE EVOLUTION OF SEX GUARDS

REVEALED SECRETS ABOUT SEX

HARTLEY MARC

Table of Contents

INTRODUCTION

The orgy is well into its fifth hour when the director finally calls, “Cut!” Almost instantly, the unbridled lust that has been crackling throughout the small adult-film set gives way to wholesale fatigue. Sweaty, naked women collapse on leather sofas and air mattresses. Men who only moments before had seemed like paragons of stamina now stagger about, spent, clumsily picking up belts, boxers, and other articles of clothing scattered about the floor. Even the film crew stretches and yawns.

In any case, the chief isn't exactly finished. "I really want another scene, folks. Furthermore, it must be hot." He looks through a knot of bodies,past probably the greatest names in American sexual entertainment and chooses a stocky,half-dressed man in a Nike cap. "Come on, Marc Help me around here."

Thus, following five hours, four ladies,also, three climaxes, even after all of his other male companions have tapped out for the day.

At the point when I previously became keen on the grown-up media outlet I was only a youthful fellow who needed to have intercourse with delightful ladies. At the point when I originally opened a pornography magazine it affirmed what I thought about ladies; they weren't so not the same as men. They were sexual animals, numerous with similar extraordinary sexual cravings as men.

Growing up, the sum total of what I had was the male perspective; it was about what I needed a lady to do to me. In finding the
pornography industry I saw the boundless possibilities of what sex can be. I'd get mine
furthermore, she'd get hers. I got into the business in 1994 and I've been working consistently from that point forward.

I shot pornography practically consistently for a year. I figured out how to keep my dick hard, my contemplations centered, and to come on command. Things that others battled with, I showed myself how to do, everyday and no matter what. First and foremost I was like any other youngster; arrogant, excited, skilled, and not entirely settled, yet without discipline. What I presently know all about is the consequence of fifteen long stretches of mental and actual discipline. It obviously didn't come for the time being. I fizzled ordinarily, and a portion of those times were destroyed. How could I return from execution disappointment? I needed to learn the most effective method to let things go.
In sex, we establish a connection rapidly,
whether it's our size, method, or stamina. In the realm of pornography I was evaluated on a lot greater scale. I was serious, large, gorgeous, and ready to screw twenty ladies in a solitary day. Then toward the finish of that day return to being simply one more person dealing with my family and living my dream. Those polarizing

universes gave me a remarkable viewpoint about what I do and what it means for individuals.

Chapter 1: A Sexual Life

Quite a while back, a married couple acquainted themselves with me at a nearby show and let me know how much they cherished my motion pictures. I was somewhat shocked that the spouse let his better half watch pornography. As though he'd guess what I might be thinking, he grinned and said, "She generally chooses your films. That is no joke." In those days I was still new to the business. I hadn't pondered couples watching pornography together. I thought just single men were the crowd for my motion pictures. I'd even believed that spouses wouldn't need their husbands watching others have intercourse. This couple appeared so "typical" and cheerful. Meeting them provided me with a superior comprehension of how pornography could connect with couples and that it had a far more extensive crowd than I had suspected.

Great Sex

Since my initial youngsters, I've engaged in sexual relations and how it affects others at the forefront of my thoughts. However, I wouldn't be familiar with extraordinary sex until numerous years after the fact. Sex fulfills a need. Incredible sex fulfills the spirit, can carry another component to a former relationship, and pull you and your accomplice closer.

Sex in a relationship is a blissful neces-sity. For the lady it makes a bond with her man that reinforces the adoration between them. For the man it supports his certainty, works on his strength in the room, and communicates his love and appreciation for his lady. Closeness is key while making progress toward a solid sexual bond that will endure the difficult stretches. It's vital to set aside the opportunity to see the value in one another and to communicate the adoration and fascination you have for one another. There is an extraordinary saying, "Anything you did to get her, keep on doing to keep her." This applies to men, yet to ladies too. It ought to be a welcome test to keep on tracking down ways of dazzling the individual you love. Extraordinary sex isn't simple when you're far off, diverted, and depleted. It takes pas-sion, time, and motivation, and that can now and again be difficult to find. Leave the issues of the world external to your entryway and invest quality energy with the one you love. "Personal time" is perfect, yet you really want "our time" too. Keeping a psychological agenda of your darling's preferences is useful. This way you generally understand what they like and can give it to them at whatever point they need it. Does the person like hot showers, blossoms, foot rubs, penis massages in the vehicle, doing it out in the open, or nestling on the love seat? Regarding and dealing with your accomplice's requirements is an essential move toward more profound, significant, incredible sex.

Men Are from Mars, Ladies Are from Venus

As verified in the well known book, people are unique, genuinely and physically. In any case, I don't believe we're different to the point that we're from discrete planets, despite the fact that our disparities now and again cause it to feel as such. Furthermore, in no spot is that distinction more prominent than in the room. For most men "fulfilling" sex is tied in with getting hard and coming, while most ladies ache for sensations of closeness and delicacy similarly as much as sexual energy. Frequently it's exceptionally simple (and normal) for a man to have fulfilling sex without addressing his darling's necessities of closeness and closeness. What we need from one another is an effective method for measuring what we can give. Men need solace, mindfulness, sympathy, and company. Ladies need mindfulness, closeness, and closeness. The lady a man picks needs to consider his identity personally and have the option to help and sustain his true capacity. The man a lady picks needs to consider her identity personally and be a mindful, physically mindful man she can converse with, who is likewise ready to fulfill her requirements.

Learn to Communicate

Everyone benefits from talking to one another, especially when it comes to sex, yet few of us feel it natural to talk about our sexual and personal preferences. By communicating these sensitive aspects of yourself to your partner, you are disclosing intimate thoughts and feelings. Men in particular find this to be uncomfortable. Guys, when having sex is the ideal moment to discuss sex. Try to be thankful, and when you are enjoying something, let your partner know what you like about it. In the manner of, "I love the way you're licking my dick. Just keep doing it that way. Asking her directly, "Do you enjoy that?" is also beneficial. Does this feel pleasant? Let her know that you like what she's doing, care about her enjoyment, and be attentive to her needs. This enables her to comprehend your preferences and the preferred methods of performance. But some guys might find it simpler to broach the subject of sex at other times, especially if they're in a relationship and don't typically discuss it in bed. When you're both at ease and having a drink or dinner, you might attempt to lightly broach the subject. Or bring it up subtly, like after you've read something or watched something similar on TV.

Learn to listen

Talking to your partner is vital, but so is listening to them. Stop what you're doing, and turn your head to look at them directly to show that you're interested in what they have to say. Be compassionate, caring, and empathic when you answer. Women frequently just need to be comforted; they don't necessarily need to be informed what they're doing incorrectly or how to improve. Sometimes all ladies want is for their man to listen to them and comprehend what they are going through. A hearty hug at this time wouldn't hurt anyone, I'm sure. Ladies, males frequently merely want you to listen to them, and most of the time they want you to concur. The timing is not now to tell your man that his employer is correct and that he is being careless.

Now is the moment to pay close attention to him. Give a sympathetic nod. Perhaps a good embrace when he's finished will be exactly what he needs.

Sex Versus Intimacy

Have you ever experienced "amazing" sex the night before only to awaken the next morning feeling unfulfilled or perhaps uneasy about the person you were sharing your bed with? You are experiencing a lack of intimacy. The previous evening, two people were looking for self-satisfaction. If you both want a one-night stand or to satisfy your own needs, there is nothing wrong with it. But if you're searching for something more in-depth, that's a different matter. Sincere affection and connection are not fleeting feelings. Only by getting to know someone and showing that you care about their wants and feelings can you accomplish these things. Don't be misled; this doesn't only relate to short-term relationships or flings; it can also occur frequently in long-term partnerships.

Instant Gratification

The five important facets of each of our lives are the physical, emotional, mental, social, and spiritual. These five components are intended to function as a unit. Our desire for rapid fulfillment is one of the difficulties. We search for an immediate fix when the demand for intimacy in a relationship is not met, frequently attempting to find it through physical proximity. Being intimate with someone is simpler on the physical level than it is in any of the other four ways. Depending on the impulse, you can get physically intimate with someone in an hour or a half. But you quickly learn that there is a much more profound desire that sex may only temporarily alleviate.

What is intimacy

Although the word intimacy has come to be associated with sexuality, it actually means much more than that. It encompasses all parts of our life, including the social, emotional, mental, and spiritual facets in addition to the physical ones. To be intimate, one must share, be honest, and be open to being hurt. Even while we crave intimacy, we frequently fear showing our vulnerability. We're all in pain. When that occurs, we shut off a portion of ourselves and make a promise to never allow it to happen again. We reduce our chances of experiencing genuine closeness and love with our spouse by doing that. Although the possibility of pain increases the closer you get to someone, our dread of pain prevents us from developing and keeping the deeper connections that we need.

What is Love?

Let me first clarify what it isn't. It's not some idyllic state when all problems, questions, and fears vanish and everything turns out well. Hollywood would have us believe that when we find "the one," everything magically becomes wonderful, but this is not how true love really is. Work is love. The giving aspect of love. Love is about comprehension. Love involves taking unconventional actions. Love is about compassion, empathy, and selflessness. Possibly not things that come naturally to us. Funny enough, although we use the phrase "falling in love," love isn't really falling until it feels like going down a flight of steps. We make love; we don't fall in love. In other words, by giving to your mate, you foster love. the greater of oneself you put into anything or anyone, the more attached you get to it or them. Although it may seem easy, doing it is challenging. To eventually realize that partnerships are not just about having all of your needs and wants satisfied, but also about selflessly addressing the needs of your partner, demands a leap of faith as well as time and effort.

Time For sex

Making time for sex is crucial, especially in long-term relationships and difficult situations. Although it may seem quite clear, we frequently take ourselves, our spouse, and our sex life for granted when we're stressed, overworked, sad, and unhappy with our lives. You might be surprised to learn that many people in long-term partnerships frequently have little to no sex or none at all for months. What irony, you spend all this time looking for the "ideal" partner, you're monogamous, and yet you're still alone. Why? Think about the strains of daily life, such as lengthy workdays, arduous commutes, a faltering economy, concerns about one's job and finances, children and duties, or even simple exhaustion. Even worse, we typically don't notice this until it's already too late.. Then, we are at a loss for what to do or, worse still, we start blaming our partner. Making time for one another is the simple fix, though. Prioritize spending time together. Sometimes, all it takes is scheduling it in. The anticipation typically disappears from sex when two people live together, whether they are married or not. Remember those beautiful early days of dating, when the anticipation of meeting up was so intense? Well, that buildup certainly makes for great sex. And even though you share the mortgage, the chores, and are allegedly able to do it whenever you want, it's difficult to recreate.

Chapter 2: someone for Everyone

ladies who are more lighthearted and have somewhat more meat on their bones, much more meat truth be told. A lot more men than ladies even accept. So feel free to become involved with the regular picture of excellence and you'll fall into the snare of concluding which men truly care about. You're responsible to be off-base, and all the more significantly, in the event that the image you've thought of is a long way from your existence, you'll stroll around regretting yourself. What's more, trust me, it'll show. Being provocative is tied in with feeling attractive. Certainty and an extraordinary character are main considerations in feeling provocative. A lady can be hot wearing old sweats or a night outfit, with her hair pulled back nonchalantly in a pig tail or salon great. She's hot while attempting to cook, while losing at b-ball yet making an honest effort. As per a ton of my female companions, a man is most provocative when he's making an effort not to be; the point at which he's attempting to change a diaper, or simply waking, looking stunned and defenseless. He's provocative while he's giggling and he's particularly hot while he's crying. Ladies find a man who can be defenseless, extremely, provocative. In this way, fellas, I realize we're educated to be hard, however now and again it's the point at which we're delicate, when we put down our walls, that we're the most adorable. In all honesty, hotness begins within first. In the event that you're not content with yourself you won't ever be provocative. Furthermore, by cheerful I don't mean a specific weight or look or status. I mean being sound, content with your work, and individuals in your day to day existence. There are straightforward things that will make you blissful and when you're cheerful, you attract individuals to you.

Beauty us in the eyes of the Beholder

What goes about adoring your business has to do with cherishing yourself? It's to a lesser extent a jump than you could suspect. We invest a great deal of energy at specific employment, or working. On the off chance that we could do without what we do, or individuals who encompass us at work, we will invest a great deal of energy being despondent. Chris Rock does an interesting mono-logue about having some work as opposed to having a profession. To reword his daily schedule, you realize you have some work when you can hardly hang tight for it to end or fear going to it and the hours haul by while you're there. You realize you have a vocation when you love what you do, can hardly stand by to get to work, and find the hours fly by while you're working. Doing the very thing you love causes you to feel approved, gives you something to anticipate, and endeavor to be great at. Furthermore, when you're enveloped with work, you basically lack opportunity and energy to fixate on your body, relationship, or deficiency in that department. People find individuals who are happy with their work simpler to be around in light of the fact that they're not continuously fussing or griping about their work, their chief, or individuals they work with.

GET OFF YOUR ASS

Practice makes you fit, sound, and makes you love your body more. Resolving supports body certainty, whether or not or not your shape changes. Being dynamic all by itself further develops self-perception — any getting down to business that happens is actually a reward. Besides, going to the exercise center provides you with a feeling of motivation, supports your endorphins, which causes you to feel significantly better and assists with dissipating gloom. The exercise center is additionally an incredible spot to meet other similar individuals.

EAT WELL

Eating great remains closely connected with dealing with your body. Practicing good eating habits assists you with detoxing and thinning and gives you energy. However, similar to working out, the advantages of eating quality food varieties go far past any impact they might have on your weight. Vegetables, organic products, entire grains, sound fats, and lean protein assist with keeping glucose steady and key chemicals in balance, the two of which straightforwardly influence your feelings. Eats less carbs wealthy in these food varieties have been related with lower rates of sadness. So assuming your temperament is better, and you feel improved, your self-perception and confidence get to the next level. Be that as it may, anything you do — this implies you, women — kindly don't begin coming down on yourself to screen and fixate on each chomp. It's a treat. You ate it. Continue on. Try not to harp on it or that large number of well meaning goals vacate the premises.

IT'S WHO YOU KNOW

As per numerous ladies I know, getting praises from different ladies helps them like and keep their shape. Encircle yourself with individuals who help you have a positive outlook on yourself.

Figure out how TO TAKE A COMPLIMENT

We make a solid attempt to look great however when somebody offers us a commendation, we promptly express something to degrade it. We wind up dismissing the acknowledgement we're searching for. Work on saying "much obliged" when somebody gives you a compli-ment. Don't overanalyze it, or judge the provider, or downplay it; rather let it absorb and permit yourself to feel better. While you're figuring out how to take a commendation, figure out how to give one too. By recognizing the positive qualities in others, you can begin to see the positive qualities in yourself. Keep in mind, to be adored you need to give love.

Try not to COMPARE

At the point when we contrast ourselves with others we get praises from different ladies to help them like and keep their shape. Encircle yourself with individuals who help you have a positive outlook on yourself.

Figure out how TO TAKE A COMPLIMENT

We make a solid attempt to look great however when somebody offers us a commendation, we generally lose. The real factors of our looks and theirs don't for a moment even matter. At the point when we take a gander at others, we perceive how wonderful they are. At the point when we take a gander at ourselves, we perceive how blemished we are. We believe we can never cut the mustard, regardless of anything else. Love the things about yourself that make you unique; your delightful hands, full mouth, wide nose, your capacity to make others giggle. There are numerous things about us that make us attrac-tive. Center around these things and not the things you believe are inadequate.

Center Around THE POSITIVES

Detesting your body can turn into a persistent vice. Figuring out how to zero in on the up-sides gives you an entire alternate point of view. Center around the positive qualities in your day to day existence. Respect the excellence of a dusk, stroll along the water, pause and enjoy the scenery. Center around what makes you delightful. Figure out how to adore your body even with the additional ten pounds. See the positive qualities in it. By pondering what's certain about ourselves we quit zeroing in on what's negative. This is something that other peo-ple get on; in the end your fulfillment with yourself attracts individuals to you.

KNOWING IS HALF THE BATTLE

Regardless of your cravings — to be restricted, shrouded in honey, or to do it outside — there's somebody who might be listening who maintains that you should do it with you. In any case, they won't ever know it on the off chance that you don't tell them. Knowing how to converse with your darling, about everything under the sun, makes a man or lady extremely hot. There's just a single method for understanding what you need and that is to examine it and to explore — not excessively far out of your usual range of familiarity, yet only without a doubt farther than you typically would go. This is significant in light of the fact that knowing is a portion of the fight. A ton of people out there are as yet looking for their Mr. or Ms. Right. I realize there is somebody who might be listening for yourself and recall that, they probably won't seem as though it from the start. A portion of the ladies I've had the best sex with are the ones I least anticipated. Simply be open and willing.

Chapter 3: what men want

I wasn't expecting sex, it simply worked out. I headed toward her home to discuss the military. She was a tactical whelp who was presently in the military and I met her at a club months prior, however we had chatted on the telephone an adequate number of times to warrant a visit. At the point when I strolled in, hip hop recordings were playing on BET. I don't have any idea why I had quit watching recordings, yet I wound up making up for lost time in them now. She plunked down close to me and inquired as to whether I'd like a beverage. She was exactly on schedule. I didn't need to consider it. We had a beverage while we watched Ray J lure some honeys. At the point when she inquired as to whether I was eager it seemed obvious to me that I was, however I didn't figure she could cook. As I expected, she had chips but no salsa. And afterward she shocked me, she was a young lady from the South, Texas to be precise, and had extras from the day preceding some grilled chicken she'd barbecued. I like my new barbecued food, yet she talked me into it. After the microwave blared she returned into the room with a major plate of food. The smell made them sit up and pay heed. Indeed, even microwaved it was heavenly. Damn, I thought, looks, disposition, and she could cook. I was in paradise. A firm beverage, a decent feast, a lovely lady; what was straightaway? Before I could complete the idea she stood up and went to her room. I watched her go, yet didn't follow. After a second she shouted to me. I strolled into her room and saw her half exposed, spread across her bed. I wasn't expecting sex, wasn't in any event, mulling over everything. Be that as it may, she'd provided every one of the makings of an essential night: great food and a lovely lady who needed to satisfy me.

A Confident Woman

What is it that men need in a lady? That is simple: great food, extraordinary sex, and a messy brain. A hot, certain lady, who can voice her terrible considerations, is a tremendous turn on. A few ladies generally tend to assume that which men need from them is: feed me, screw me, and shut the fuck up. What most men truly need is to feed me, screw me, and speak profanely to me. With sex, all hindrances ought to vacate the premises. You're bare, he's exposed — no sense in being unassuming at this point. Let it out, voice your longings. Speaking profanely isn't a wrongdoing, regardless of your mother's thought process. In the event that you feel it, make it happen, and in the event that you like it, say it. In the intensity of a decent fuck, you will express the things you were just reasoning a moment back. Most ladies don't appear to comprehend that communicating their thoughts physically is additionally engaging. It tells a man how you feel and what you need to feel. You can begin by discussing a dream or simply a sexual encounter you once had. In the event that you're terrified to share those private sentiments, make up a tale about a companion, however it's truly about you and get imaginative in the subtleties. Men come in different types; they can be free and agreeable or firmly twisted and controlled, however they all need to develop and impart their sexual longings to the lady they're having intercourse to. The greater part of us don't get out whatever we feel inspired by a paranoid fear of judgment or kickback. However, in the cozy and confidential setting of sex, a couple of dangers are very much compensated. A lot of men, and ladies, have similar grimy contemplations with regards to sex. From my experience, ladies have an undeniably more unequivocal brain. Simply investigate pornography; the most famous entertainers are the ones who do everything — butt-centric, trios, pack bangs, servitude and accommodation, endlessly. As the remainder of the world disregards the sexual social butterfly, furtively a couple are observing. Ladies set a model that men can seldom follow; they hold the ability to switch him off and turn him on. Speaking profanely and being interesting will give your accomplice thoughts he hadn't contemplated previously and on the off chance that he's a genuine man he'll see the value in it. Those considerations and thoughts can now be transformed right into it. Let's assume you have a timid person, you've taken care of him and presently you will screw him. Speaking profanely can relax him. A couple of very much picked words can deliver him once again from his shell. Presently don't terrify him, allure him. Or on the other hand even better, perhaps placing a little trepidation into him will get you what you're searching for. For a decent fuck, a few men need an instructing lady, or even a lady who understands what she needs and how to get it. That's what genuine men regard. It's acceptable for a lady to assume command, to physically guide her man. Simply don't be bossy. I know it's a barely recognizable difference to be commanding and hot, and it takes practice. However, attempt it; you'll be amazed at the outcomes. Scandalous talk can go two different ways. A few words can be utilized to incite a man to feel tested to screw harder or better than anyone might have expected and you can mellow others by leisurely removing what makes a feline not do how he truly needs to treat you. That is what men need, a lady to draw out the best in him. X-appraised conversations can have far-running outcomes. I'm continually shocked by the number of individuals that bring a one of a kind sexual knowledge to the table for that I hadn't considered or even considered. That is the reason imparting what you need, particularly with the perfect individual, is vital to having a sound and compensating sexual coexistence. A lady who can genuinely communicate that won't just have her pick of darlings, however will likewise have a superior under-remaining of herself.

Good Food

The platitude "The method for monitoring's heart is through his stomach" is flawless. Your man believes that you should take care of him. I couldn't say whether men favor great cooking to great sex, yet I realize no man can turn down a decent dinner. I've gotten back home following a long hard day and been revived to track down a hot feast. Realizing that somebody adequately minded to get some margin to cook for me generally fills my heart with joy so much better, and makes me considerably more grateful. Keep in mind, cooking for your man is additionally a valuable chance to more deeply study what he appreciates and how to fulfill him. One significant hint: assuming this is the principal dinner you're making for him, keep it straightforward. Adhere to a simple recipe that you know he will cherish. Despite the fact that he'll see the value in the idea regardless of how the food ends up, you would rather not undermine yourself by picking something excessively convoluted. Whenever you've picked your recipe, ensure you invest the same amount of energy setting up the scene and it is just about as heartfelt as conceivable to ensure the setting. An extraordinary feast can be made multiple times more heartfelt by eating it in an erotic climate, and a candlelit table and delicate music are similarly pretty much as significant as a decent dinner. Astonishing him with a heartfelt feast in bed or when he returns home for lunch or supper is really smart, in spite of the fact that it could take some anticipating your part. Be that as it may, assuming that it's your most memorable time in the kitchen, why not request that he cook the feast with you? Cooking together is a great method for getting to know one another and have some good times simultaneously. When you attempt it you'll likely believe that you should rehash it. Each lady can make a dinner of some kind or another. The relationship that exists between a decent dinner and great sex is a personal one. Men are exceptionally quick to the detail that goes into arranging a dinner, they know it's a wonderful source of both blessing and pain, not something you need to do, it's something you need to do, and sex ought to be the same way.

Tips for a Romantic Meal

BE SPONTANEOUS.

A heartfelt feast can be significantly more unique in the event that it's a shock. Just take my word for it, he'll be significantly more grateful to get back home to a scrumptious dinner in a magnificent setting when it appears unexpectedly.

Set up YOUR MEAL TOGETHER.

Looking for and preparing a dinner together can likewise be an extraordinary method for interfacing. If you both have the opportunity, meet after work at the supermarket, choose the fixings, and cook the feast together.

Have a go at SOMETHING DIFFERENT. In the event that you generally eat pasta or chicken, have a go at making steak or fish. It will be a much needed development from the standard dinner.

DRESS THE PART. Try not to only spruce up for supper, likewise spruce in the mood for cooking. A hot culinary expert's outfit, mischievous house cleaner's uniform, or wearing his number one undergarments will make everything look and taste that greatly improved.

KEEP IT SIMPLE.

Try not to deplete yourself by cooking an excessively intricate multi course feast with fixings it took you the entire day to find. Keep the dinner basic so you can both really appreciate it from start to finish. Restrict yourself to a serving of mixed greens or simple starter and a fundamental course with a fast side dish.

Remember

DESSERT. Pastry can be the most awesome aspect of the dinner, and can continuously be worked off later. Once more, keep it straightforward. You would rather not be so exhausted subsequent to making a debilitating dinner and sweet that you drop before your man can appropriately much obliged. A most loved straightforward pastry is delectable ready strawberries plunged in liquefied chocolate. I suggest these be made ahead of time so they can cool. Then, at that point, you should simply whip them out of the cooler.

APHRODISIACS A Spanish fly is a substance accepted to increment sexual craving or make sex more pleasurable. The name comes from Aphrodite, the Greek goddess of exotic nature. Despite the fact that there is no clinical proof that aphrodisiacs really work, they can be loads of fun to plan and eat together.

ARTICHOKES. The basic demonstration of stripping an artichoke of its leaves, dunking them into margarine, and scratching off the delicate tissue with your teeth is an extremely sexy encounter. Essentially cut off the artichoke's prickly tips, snap off the intense leaves, cut off the stem, and rub with lemon juice. Steam until delicate, around thirty to an hour. Have a go at plunging artichokes into curried mayonnaise, lemon or spice margarine, or vinaigrette.

ASPARAGUS. Given its phallic shape, asparagus is much of the time delighted in as a Spanish fly food. Feed your sweetheart bubbled or steamed lances plunged in spread, olive oil, or hollandaise sauce for an erotic encounter. The Vegetarian Society recommends "eating asparagus for three days for the most impressive impact."

ALMONDS. These nuts have been an image of fruitfulness all through the ages. The fragrance is remembered to prompt energy in a lady. Take a stab at serving marzipan (almond glue) looking like organic products for an extraordinary after supper treat.

AVOCADO. This is a delightful organic product with an exotic surface. Served in cuts with a limited quantity of balsamic vineg

BANANAS. The banana has a hot phallic shape that is to some extent liable for why it is viewed as a sexual enhancer. All the more essentially, bananas are plentiful in potassium and B nutrients, necessities for sex chemical creation.

BASIL (SWEET BASIL). This spice is said to invigorate the sex drive and lift fruitfulness. Delivering a general feeling of prosperity for body and mind is likewise known. Serve new basil leaves over mozzarella, tomatoes, and olive oil for an invigorating and simple plate of mixed greens.

CHOCOLATE.

Chocolate has phenylethylamine and serotonin, two synthetic compounds that light up joy regions in the cerebrum. It likewise contains synthetics remembered to influence synapses in the cerebrum and a connected substance to caffeine and theobromine. Chocolate contains more cell reinforcements (malignant growth forestalling chemicals) than red wine. The mystery for enthusiasm is to join the two. Attempt a glass of cabernet with a touch of dull chocolate for an exotic treat.

CARROTS. These vegetables are high in nutrients and beta-carotene and carrots are accepted to be a male energizer. The phallus-formed carrot has likewise been related with feeling since old times and was utilized by early Middle Eastern eminence to help temptation. On the off chance that you and your man like carrots, attempt carrot cake or even carrot cake cupcakes for dessert. On the off chance that you like smoothies, you can juice a carrot and add it to your morning smoothie.

Espresso. Caffeine is a notable energizer yet recollects, to an extreme and it turns into a depressant. Espresso invigorates both the body and the psyche so a short while after supper assists you with conquering the languor of an extraordinary feast and sets you up for a dusk 'til dawn affair. Attempt a modest quantity of rich dim espresso with dessert or with just enough dim chocolate you can take care of one another.

FIGS. These natural products are considered a sexual energizer, maybe in light of the fact that an open fig seems to be the female sex organs. Tearing open a fig and eating it before your sweetheart can be exceptionally provocative. Serve new figs in a pleasant bowl and make certain to eat them with your fingers.

GARLIC. The intensity in garlic is said to mix sexual longings. Garlic has been utilized for quite a long time to fix everything from the normal cold to heart trouble. Use it with some restraint and ensure you and your darling offer it together. Appreciate pasta thrown with a delicately garlicky sauce and it might prompt something hot in the room later.

GINGER. Ginger Root, crude, cooked, or solidified, is an energizer to the circulatory framework. A pan fried food with newly ground ginger is a straightforward, delectable, and fun dinner you can plan together.

HONEY. Many drugs in old Egypt depended on honey, including solutions for sterility and feebleness. Middle age enticers took care of their sweethearts mead, a matured beverage produced using honey. There are numerous ways of utilizing honey — sprinkled over frozen yogurt, in tea, or later, on your darling in the room. MUSTARD. This spice is accepted to animate the sexual organs and in-wrinkle want. A dish or steak with a mustard and peppercorn sauce and a plate of mixed greens is a basic, scrumptious, and filling dinner that won't make you excessively lazy for the sake of entertainment later on.

NUTMEG. This zest was exceptionally valued by Chinese ladies as a Spanish fly. In enormous amounts nutmeg can deliver a stimulating result. A light sprinkling in a warm pumpkin soup can assist with brightening up your night. Nutmeg sprinkled over a warm foamy cappuc-cino could likewise get the job done. Clams. These shellfish were archived as aphrodisiacs by the Romans. It presumably doesn't hurt that the clam looks like the female privates. Truly clams are nutritious, high in protein, easy to get ready, and delectable.

PINE NUTS. Zinc is a vital mineral important to keep up with male power and pine nuts are wealthy in zinc. Pine nuts have been utilized to animate the moxie as far back as bygone eras. Delightful pine nut treats with coffee make for an invigorating pastry. PINEAPPLE. Plentiful in L-ascorbic acid, pineap-ples are utilized as a homeopathic treat-ment for weakness. Add a lance to a sweet rum beverage for a delectable introduction to a night of enthusiasm. Indeed, even canned cubed pineapples eaten with tooth-picks are a basic, however reviving sweet.

RASPBERRIES AND STRAWBERRIES. These berries are ideal food sources for hand-taking care of your sweetheart. Both are high in L-ascorbic acid and make a sweet light pastry. Or on the other hand add whipped cream for a more provocative treat. TRUFFLES. The Greeks and the Romans considered the intriguing truffle mushroom to be a sexual enhancer. The musky aroma is said to invigorate and sharpen the skin to contact. However they can be costly and are to some degree a mixed bag, simple to find truffle oil showered over pasta and finished off with shaved Parmesan or Romano cheddar is tasty and simple to get ready.

VANILLA. The fragrance and kind of vanil-la is accepted to increase desire. Fill tall champagne glasses to the edge and add a vanilla bean for an exciting, effervescent treat. A couple of drops of vanilla concentrate in a mug of coffee is a twofold treat. WINE. Individuals have been utilizing liquor to animate their moxie for quite a long time. Yet, while a moderate measure of liquor will diminish nervousness and delivery hindrances, one glass too many is bound to make it lights-out time for you than put you in that frame of mind. Wine unwinds and assists with animating our faculties. Drinking wine can be a sensual encounter as you relish the taste all the rage and on your sweetheart's.

Regards. There isn't anything hotter than that. Regarding your darling, it is one more extraordinary Spanish fly to figure out their necessities. Sex need not generally be focused on fucking and coming. There are different ways of satisfying your darling physically. The most significant sexual connections start with deference. Attempt it; it very well may be a genuine turn-on.

Good Company

I think all men like a lady with a funny bone. Ladies who are sufficiently fortunate to be honored with insight and mind are pretty much as interesting as an ideal pearl, and men know it. Any lady who can giggle at a test or ease up a temperament will help a relationship and the sibling who views himself fortunate enough as with such a lady will have help in conquering the difficulties that face many driven men. While you're attempting to entice your man, have a go at being senseless. It can likewise be a colossal turn-on. A tough lady makes her man more grounded. Her comical inclination will help him to remember the entertaining side of things while he's inclination low and give him a much needed boost. Downplaying what is happening takes expertise and magnetism, however certified giggling is the award. Humor resounds and helps us to remember our humanness. It removes a portion of the earnestness from life and permits us to unwind and partake in the occasion. I like when I'm with a gathering of ladies and they're open with each other. It shows me that ladies have a significant number of similar issues as men, however they have a funny bone about it that is clever, and they converse with each other about everything. That way they can get alternate points of view and understanding that assists them with their concerns. To all you all out there who figure you can't converse with ladies, since you don't grasp them: Listen, sibling, it's this straightforward — simply inspire her to let out a smirk. It'll put you both on a shared view. It's something very similar with us men — it makes us giggle. Offer us a major hot grin like you're offering newly heated treats. Share your cheerful dispositions and your chuckling. It'll come off on us and make us need to accompany you.

SINGLE MEN

Single men are somewhat unique in relation to wedded men, however they share large numbers of similar necessities, for example, having somebody to impart time to. At the point when you're single, contingent upon how far you're arranging into the future, your objective is basically to have somebody accessible when you need her. She ought to be pretty and provocative enough to make your young men offer you the go-ahead. Past that it's each day in turn. Obviously a ton really relies on how you were raised and your family foundation, yet most men in their twenties aren't contemplating long haul connections. They're living at this point. That is the reason they're many times less able to change for their young lady, since, think about what, there are a lot of different ladies out there. It's not until they mature a bit and comprehend what the perfect lady brings to their lives do they understand that there are similarly numerous men out there and that the ideal lady merits the split the difference. We men hear so frequently about ladies managing men who will not commit and just need to fuck. Assuming he's young and narrow minded that might be his main desire, however it could be her desire also. Nothing bad can be said about it, in the event that it's common. On the off chance that you need more than that, perhaps he's not the best person for you. In any case, to know that you both need to impart, which doesn't generally come simple when you're in your twenties. At the point when you're single with nobody to think often about except for yourself, you will generally be more childish. This applies to youthful single ladies too. We ought to understand what we're getting into. Be clear about what we need and afterward offer to one another what we need as a trade off. I'll tell the truth, when I was a youthful, sin-gle buddy all I needed to do was fuck (don't snicker . . .because I can read your mind), yet what I need from ladies presently is totally different from what I needed in those days. Now that I'm more established and have a family, my perspectives are unique. I need a lady who is sufficiently free to deal with things when I can't. I like my lady streetwise and ready to deal with herself on the off chance that I'm not ready to show up for her. I need a lady who can show me things, push me, yet cause me to feel like I'm unique. To the women, don't lose trust in the more youthful years. Single men might partake in their opportunity and would like it to remain as such, however over the long run he might adjust his perspective. My young lady stayed by me through various challenges, had an effect when it was essential, and affected me. What's more, being a decent cook didn't do any harm, all things considered.

Hitched MEN

At the point when you're hitched your necessities change, and men end up pondering keeping a relationship, having an accomplice in life for that large number of troublesome times. Marriage significantly affects a man that could conceivably do him great. It relies upon assuming that he picks the right accomplice. In the event that you track down a blissful spouse, it's most likely protected to figure his significant other is cheerful too. In those cases it would be the consistent sustaining or the strength of somebody sure and consoling. Eventually men need to experience harmony, quiet, and agreement in their home and with their better half. This assists with calming all the clamor that is happening outside the relationship, at work, with their rela-tives, or in any of the many things we need to manage day to day. So it was nothing unexpected that when I asked married men what they needed most from their connection ships they generally said harmony, so they can take it with them out into the world.

Support

When I initially began pondering which men needed, I contemplated what I needed. I came to acknowledge I'd for a long time needed love, regard, and backing. I realize trust is hard to acquire. I don't request it; I desire to procure it through my activities. Due to my unique capacity to frustrate here and there, I center around my assets and not my shortcomings. So I give what I hope to get. From a lady I anticipate love, and on the grounds that we're in the same boat and we've settled on a cognizant choice to go down this way, I likewise anticipate her help. As a man raising a family, her help is vital and it's essential for progress. I genuinely accept that the greater part of us men hope to need to make penances to bring about some benefit for the relationship, and we anticipate that our ladies should do likewise. Trust is a singular choice; I don't figure you can genuinely believe somebody until you know their personality, until you've seen them under unfriendly circumstances. How would they treat you in critical circumstances or in unfa-vorable conditions? For me that is a decent measure, yet it's not the most ideal one all of the time. Since when times are great and promising it's not difficult to be adoring, mindful, and delicate. Sadly, in life things turn out badly. Our lives are a mix of victories and disappointments. You lose that gig, you don't receive that pay increase, or you're feeling like this masculinity thing is a significant weight to bear. Men need — no, men need basic reassurance in their daily existences. The help of a decent lady can make going through those things simpler. She can facilitate the weight of being a hawker, a supplier, and at times of being a daddy. We don't anticipate that you should comprehend all that we're going through. In some cases just the fellas can offer a couple of useful tidbits, yet your support and consolation certainly quiets the burdens of our hustle. A lady's understanding has consistently had an impact in our capacity to see past our difficulties and put things into viewpoint. Her words can have an effect on the way we see the world. I have confidence for you women: giving a man what he needs isn't dependably what he quite; a lady who realizes this is far on the ball.

Mutual Appreciation

What I believe ladies should leave with subsequent to pursuing this part is that however it might appear we men are miserable, don't surrender in light of the fact that with experience comes understanding. The more we get to realize each other the more we can see the value in what we both bring to the relationship. A portion of the development men need to arrange life we can get from our ladies. It might take men longer to see the value in how a lady helps him and that can be credited to his past connections, youth, or childhood. We each have something extraordinary that drives us, figures out what our identity is, and characterizes us as individuals. A lady who can see the value in our peculiarities and peculiarities improves things significantly in the existence of the man she is engaged with. In your relationship make changes; get to realize the individual you've decided to invest energy with. Celebrate what makes

them extraordinary, appreciate their characteristics as exceptional and shared as confidential among you. What a man needs most is acknowledgment, to be cherished for what his identity is. In the event that you have a decent man, a remarkable man, he will move himself to be preferable over he is.

Tune In and Turn On

Presently, it doesn't matter to me how great you cook. In the event that it's not cooking among you in the room, it won't stand the test of time. Yet, how would you provide him with that kind of sex that leaves him hungry for more? How might you secure him down in the room, you inquire? Physically, we as a whole have a button that when pushed draws out the oddity in us. For the fortunate rare sorts of people who find somebody willing and ready to press that button we never need to leave the person in question. Frequently, it's seriously straightforward. I have a companion who loves ass fucking. His young lady additionally loves to get screwed in the ass. That's the short and long of it? I like a charming ass in a short skirt. My young lady has the most gorgeous ass and she adores wearing short skirts for me. Once in a while the most essential things will make a man want more and more. Beside that, it's your certainty, sexual and in any case. I decipher certainty as accomplishing something well and having a damn decent outlook on it. Being certain will establish a connection with a man like clockwork. Whether it's pad talk, being an incredible cook, or basically fucking him into fatigue. Remain one stride in front of his longings, giving him what he wants, even before he realizes he wants it. That can be a foot rub, a cushion, a bite, or a sensual caress. In any event, sprucing up like a stripper or taking him to a strip club. Being with a tuned lady into your sentiments is consistently the greatest turn-on.

BE TRUE TO YOURSELF

Albeit this section is about which men need, it's likewise about what a lady can, or will, give. Regardless of the amount you might need to be the lady your man maintains that you should be, being consistent with yourself is imperative. To fulfill him without losing yourself or feeling not exactly entire, since, say, you're not the best cook, joke-teller, or homemaker. Regardless of anything else, I've found the ladies I like the most have been the most authentic and reliable. In this manner they've brought me over to their approach to being. In this way, she's not making me a four-course dinner and we're requesting all things considered and it's the best feast ever on the grounds that we're having it together.

Men need to make sure to get what they need from a lady — love, constancy, trust, earnestness, appreciation — something they are likewise able to give.

Chapter 4: What Women Want

My head's down, my girl's close by, and I'm stepping hard through the heated products segment of the neighborhood Ralph's, attempting to finish my handbasket and make it up there in time for an individual appearance I have in a couple of hours. I'm so engaged, I nearly miss this beautiful Latin lady checking out at me from the far edge of the path. She's remaining with a kid about my little girl's age. She's wearing some close Guess pants and a perfectly sized white T-shirt. Her lipstick matches the pink finish on the toenails looking from her shoes. Her hair is pulled back in a braid. Our eyes met, and I delayed a bit. I say nothing. I simply walk around her and visually connect. I grin, slant my head rapidly, and continue onward. In my mind, I'm doing some friendly math, attempting to figure out the reason why she's looking at me. Does she know me from my movies? Did I meet her at a party somewhere? Is it safe to say that she is simply sprung on a sibling? What? I do a couple of additional goes through the walkways, sure to pass by any place I see her. Each time, I look at her and continue moving, still not letting out the slightest peep, simply checking her mind-set and conveying my own. I can't rush — not on the off chance that I need the pussy. While attempting to meet a lady in a public spot, a man certainly needs to check his energy before he takes action. You must be certain that you're getting the appropriate sig-nals. Now and again, that obviously sug-gestive eye to eye connection you'd swear you two made is simply, to her psyche, just cordial looks. Assuming you're intrigued, don't take her for a little look. Look close at the lady. Check whether she's actually a darling you need. Note what turns you on about her: Is it her walk, her legs, her bosoms, or her grin? Consider how she answers, as well. Is it true that she is grinning? Do her eyes sell out any interest in your past "For what reason is this man taking a gander at me so hard?" If she's likewise looking at you, what is she checking out? Is it your hair, your arms, your shoes, or your groin? What-ever it is, be cool about it and let her eyes wander all they need. On the lookout, I give her one final look and grin and afterward I head for the checkout counter. Similarly as I step in line I hear a voice behind me, "Your little girl's charming." I pivot to see the lady driving her truck into the line. I grin and say thanks to her, my most memorable words since we recognized one another. I then, at that point, offer her my spot in the long queue. (The better to see her butt, as well, yet I don't see a lot of motivation to tell her that . . . I figure she knows at this point.) Standing straightforwardly behind her, I draw near. Then, at that point, in a soft tone, I tell her how great she smells, then I ask her name. She answers Elena and we start a little discussion. My girl heads out to play with her child close to the gumball machines at the front of the market. The line moves gradually, however Elena is moving significantly more slowly, until I'm basically finding her as I attempt to stay away from the truck behind me. I smile however I don't do aerobics. I simply stand there unobtrusively, allowing her body to contact mine softly. I've expressed around twenty words to Elena, yet that is all's enough until further notice. Before we head out in different directions I request her number, which she provides for me. I called her that evening. After two days, we have the first of incalculable sexual experiences.

Game

Ladies love style. At the point when somebody has a remarkable methodology, ladies answer. To stand apart from the pack, you need to have style. I realize ladies can appear to be threatening to the typical man. His words can fail to attract anyone's attention and his activities slip through the cracks. All that can change with a change in mental disposition. You should have the certainty to get what you need, yet first know precisely the exact thing it is that you need. Moving toward a lady is a two-way road. It offers ladies the consideration they look for and men the certainty they need to get different things throughout everyday life. It's the game we play with each other to keep life fascinating and testing, sexual and moving. At the point when I see a lady I'm drawn to, I do a little perception. Could it be said that she is forlorn, upset, responsive, far off, or congenial? I express those things since when I meet somebody, I want to work on their mind-set. I maintain that our discussion should be significant and edifying. Yet, I likewise need to establish a long term connection. Having an extraordinary methodology with just enough style goes quite far in accomplishing this. In the event that she's feeling awful, I'll attempt to make her giggle. That is consistently an extreme one on the grounds that being interesting is difficult. You risk the opportunity of not being interesting and scrambling to track down a recuperation. That's what ladies notice, so it's ideal to be entertaining provided that it falls into place without a hitch for you. Acting naturally is greatly improved. Anything your assets are, use them. Ladies are drawn to your certainty. On the off chance that you know yourself, you can utilize your assets to attract ladies to you. I like to make individuals snicker, so I attract them by being amusing or sharing something hilarious. It loosens up them and cuts down their walls. I'm a sexual feline, and on occasion I end up participated in discussions about sex. That is my solidarity and I'm edified as well as intrigued by what others need to say regarding sex. So I have two things in support of myself, sex and humor, points that make the world go around. Eventually I can entice ladies who need to be lured. Actions speak louder than words and activities are costly, so be frugal with your moves. Make it common on the off chance that you're in the prevailing position. Chill and let her run crap for some time. This reassures her. Being tempting not just carries her nearer to you, it likewise gives you a benefit in the room. Keep on making that equivalent interest in the room. In the event that you wind up assuming a part, play it without limit. Most of the ladies I realize will cooperate. It's likely what they find appealing about you and will captivate them to continue to give you what you need. I have no extraordinary lines, yet I really do have resources: my grin and my accommodating way. These have been created over the course of the years out of encounters with numerous dif-ferent individuals. Show me we are in general human, nothing unprecedented about anybody, yet something phenomenal about everybody.

Being positive and agreeable likewise assists manage dismissal or disillusionments, and downplays the negative contemplations. So consistently put in your absolute best effort. Live at the time. Try not to cause circumstances that hold you back from living without limit. At the point when I initially meet a lady, I profound search in her eyes. I need to check whether her look is open and inviting or monitored and careful. I'm not concealing anything and I genuinely want to believe that they aren't all things considered. On the off chance that there's a wall, it's cool. Over the long run we can become OK with one another. Assuming it's somebody I see as visually captivating, I ordinarily know right away on the off chance that it can go further. They say ladies know from the moment they take a gander at you on the off chance that they'll screw you. So remain on the prepared, be fly, have certainty and a lot of style, be it easygoing, cool, hot, or sure. The maxim "Garments don't make the man, the man makes the garments," is valid. Wear your garments with certainty. This is valid for all kinds of people. At the point when I get up in the first part of the day and get dressed, that is all there is to it; I'm focused on the thing I'm wearing. I consider it once I'm out. Will the garments help or hurt my demeanor? Could I at any point achieve my objectives in the thing I'm wearing? Whenever you've responded to those inquiries, continue on. You ought to have the option to stay sure on the off chance that you're wearing a T-shirt and pants or formal attire. I go to a ton of spots alone. I don't go with a gang or escort. For quite a while growing up I was alone kid, so I discovered a real sense of reconciliation in being without help from anyone else. In any case, it very well may be hard moving toward a lady, in any event, being who I am, without the positive rein-forcement of a group. You begin to ponder, Do I look great? Do I smell alright? Is there anything in my teeth? What do you do when those contemplations spring up in your mind? Keep them there. Depend on your resources. One of my best resources is that I'm patient. I can trust that a lady will come to me. At the point when they do (on the grounds that I'm grinning, easygoing, and certain), I enjoy the benefit on the grounds that the tension is on them to dazzle me. Live at the time; assuming it's great for you, there will be little you can do to really mess it up. On the off chance that it's not intended to be, it's alright because there will be different times and different ladies. Continuously stay calm and composed and continue on with beauty and certainty. Keep in mind, enticement is being attractive with certainty. Act naturally and remember to grin.

A Good Lover

Fellas, I trust this won't shock you however ladies need a decent darling. I'm certain you're all gesturing your heads, "Definitely, that's what I got," yet what makes a man a decent darling may not be your thought process. Ladies believe that you should focus in bed, focusing on them, and in addition to the demonstration. They believe that you should get familiar with their preferences and practice what you've realized. Throughout the long term I've advanced new things from various ladies. Each darling shows you something, whether it's fortunate or unfortunate. The experience leaves you with better information on yourself and understanding of your sweetheart. While a huge piece of being a decent sweetheart is having the option to fulfill your accomplice's feelings, you likewise need to keep the relationship invigorating by investigating different sexual exercises and grasping different sexual subtleties and wants. Keeping sexual connections invigorating and moving is one explanation I'm composing this book. I learned from the get-go that pornography could motivate sexual trial and error. A couple watching pornography together may find the follows up on screen a piece scaring, however the advantages of taking a stab at something new may improve darlings out of the two of them. Something men need to comprehend is that ladies need to be erotic as well as sexual. The strokes and the kisses, the holding of foreplay are pretty much as significant as how hard you can get or how long you can go. I like to involve contact to show love as well as sexual excitement. An embrace or a kiss doesn't need to be a preface to sex; it can just say I appreciate being with you. In all honesty, men appreciate being held, touched, and kissed as much as ladies. How often have you embraced your darling in the past 24 hours? We as a rule embrace an old buddy or somebody we haven't seen for a spell, at this point we seldom embrace the individual we're having intercourse with. An embrace not just energizes contacting and kissing, it likewise makes a sexy association. That association establishes the climate for foreplay and incredible sex. Here's something to attempt: stand near your darling, so close you can contact one another, however don't. Inhale gradually together, bring your lips close and partake in one another's breath. Take a stab at breathing together in a similar musicality and speed. Investigate each other's eyes, move your hands over one another's body without contacting. Keep a consistent eye to eye connection. Remain nearby, permitting your body and mind to partake in one another's space. This makes sexual pressure. At last when you do contact, make a game out of it like you are attempting to spell a word or draw an image. Keep eye to eye connection and allow it to be about the touch. Erotic contacting shows friendship, cultivates closeness, and makes sexual excitement. These are everything that ladies like.

TURNING HER OUT

From my encounters invigorating a lady's clit, either with your fingers or your mouth, is an effective method for inspiring them to come. Nonetheless, my casual overview lets me know that these are procedures that most men are not exceptionally gifted at. At the point when I'm with my woman I like to let her let me know what's working for her. She understands her body better compared to I do, what feels better, how hard I ought to rub, and where I ought to rub, so I like to follow her. Women, feel free to make some noise, your man doesn't necessarily in all cases have any idea what he's doing, regardless of whether he has the apparatuses to satisfy you, tell him the best way to utilize those devices the correct way on you. Zina Rartley is an old buddy of mine from the business with a ton of involvement. Whenever I first worked with her, she painstakingly directed me to do precisely every thing she believed me should do. This urged me to attempt an alternate strategy, since she gave me trust in its outcomes. Taking care of business I know how difficult and impervious to fundamentally altering our ways we can be. I propose finding a typical sexual objective, one that is far off for the both of you, yet with the confirmation to your lady that you can arrive at that objective together. Find a dream that energizes her and one that intrigues you too. Propose a portion of the things you'll have to get it going. Be that as it may, how would you train an old canine to do new deceives, women? Offer him treats. Ini-tially, the prize ought to be overpowering, similar to a penis massage during a Lakers game, or a tasty feast served in his number one hot outfit. In the case of nothing else, this will urge him to answer your sexual ideas. Assist your man with satisfying you by offering direction, delicately and affectionately, and giving him heaps of consolation and appreciation. Guide his hand to the spot that turns you on the most. Assist him with understanding what's excessively hard or not hard enough. Direct him on the most proficient method to rub or animate you, and make certain to tell him as well as to show him that you like what he's doing — groan, squirm, and empower him. Contingent upon what sort of feline you're with, you might need to be smooth to inspire him to do specific things. Move your body to where you believe his hands should follow. Change your hips or revolve them in a manner that invigorates you and tells him the best way to turn you on. Your clit is a delicate region, yet I've gained for a fact it can likewise become uninterested and unmotivated. Contact is significant while invigorating the clitoral region, so persistence and responsiveness is critical to doing it effectively. Being vocal in the room could switch a few people off; while others will cherish the way that you're guiding him. At the point when I believe that a young lady should improve in the area of giving me head, I praise her on the thing she's doing and afterward propose how she can improve. In the event that a lady takes a gander at me for endorsement or to perceive how answering she's doing, I express the thing I'm feeling by groaning, or licking my lips and rotating my hips. I additionally prefer to give her a portion of the joy she's giving me. A few ladies like to have their bosoms kneaded while giving head or their hair stroked, some even like being conversed with in a corrupting manner. Nothing bad can be said about calling her a frightful bitch, on the off chance that she enjoys it. Speaking profanely during sex keeps your brain off things you don't have to contemplate, and keeps you zeroed in on the main job.

A Recap of What Women Want

1. LOVE. Ladies aren't not the same as men in this division. They need somebody who is dedicated, who loves them for what their identity is, not for who they maintain that they should be. Like men they will attempt to hold tight when they think they've tracked down Mr. Right.

2. A MAN WHO IS ATTRACTIVE TO THEM. More often than not it's not necessary to focus on super strong abs. Like men, a lady needs a man who invests wholeheartedly in his ap-pearance, however not really a man who is generally at the exercise center or continuously checking out at himself in the mirror.

3. A MAN THEY CAN TRUST. Ladies need somebody they can have confidence in, who will show up for them at the end of the day. Not all men are trust-commendable or dedicated. So many, as a matter of fact, that ladies are progressively watchful. I don't genuinely accept that a lady at any point truly excuses a man who has been faithless. Like men they would rather not stress over where he's going or what he's doing. They're searching for a man they can trust.

4. A HOME LIFE. Ladies are searching for a man who will cooperate with them, who they can make arrangements for the future with. Men who are socially associated can be alluring on the grounds that they are engaging in a drawn out relationship, however they must put the home life first and add to keeping it requested and blissful.

5. Closeness. Ladies need a man who knows when to screw them and when to simply hold them. They need a man who they can converse with about everything. Somebody who gets them and who they can be transparent with. Great sex is improved by closeness; when you realize your accomplice like you know yourself.

6. A MAN WHO IS GENTLE AND KIND. These are the characteristics that would likewise make him an extraordinary dad. I'm not recommending that the lady herself needs fathering, however some do. Ladies need a man who might be an incredible fa-ther to their youngsters.

7. A MAN WITH A SENSE OF HUMOR. Ladies like men who can chuckle at themselves and at life. I know it's hard out there, fellas. Try not to figure your lady doesn't have the foggiest idea about that, as well. It's the capacity to change what you can and disregard what you might that will at any point keep you pushing ahead.

8. A MAN WHO IS STRONG AND SENSITIVE. In spite of the fact that ladies like men who are masculine, they like men who are additionally delicate. They need a man whose shoulder they can cry on yet who can likewise cause them to feel like it's all going to be okay. A man who will not chas-tise them for being personal yet who will uphold them and give them their ear when they need to talk. You folks can blow up and say, "I'm a man, she can go cry to her sweethearts," and she might do that, however she probably won't return. There are a wide range of men out there, they can pick one who can push the limit between being masculine and mindful. 9. A

MAN WHO IS SUPPORTIVE. Numerous men rush to condemn ladies about their way of behaving or profession, then approach attempting to change and form them. This won't ever work. One, you ought to be with somebody who you like basically how they are or alternately it's difficult as far as possible. Second, ladies see their rela-tionship as an emotionally supportive network, one that ought to work the two different ways. On the off chance that a man can't or is able to give that help, and rushes to condemn, he will lose his lady.

10. A MAN WHO DOESN'T HAVE TO SHOUT. Ladies need a man who can discuss, examine, and see all sides of a contention. Correspondence is similarly basically as significant as sex and similarity in a relationship. A hot enthusiastic attitude might have made you intriguing and testing at the very first moment. Yet, assuming that this is all you're giving your lady she will leave depleted and find somebody more quiet and understanding.

11. A CHALLENGING MAN. Somebody who keeps them alert and aware. At the point when tested, the best lady will adapt to the situation, frequently astounding them-selves more than their man who realized she had it in her all along. The best men draw out the best in their ladies. They show them what they are prepared to do and they reward them with expressions of help, love, and fondness when they achieve their objectives. If you have any desire to keep your lady between ested, keep her (tenderly) tested.

12. A MAN WHO WILL COMMIT TO THEM. I don't know one lady who hasn't been wounded by a man. Be

that as it may, ladies actually need a man they can impart to and trust and open up to. Very much like a man, it's difficult for a lady to give her heart, to be open and mindful, and to set out her shield of self-insurance, to be uncovered and vulner-capable. When she does that she's given you everything. There's no returning from that point. Assuming you mistreat her, she might in all likelihood won't ever recuperate.

13. Generally IMPORTANT, WOMEN DON'T WANT TO BE ALONE. This is the principal reason that when they think they've found a man who has a large number of the characteristics they need, need, and promotion soil, they're so frequently able to resolve things.

www.ingramcontent.com/pod-product-compliance
Lightning Source LLC
LaVergne TN
LVHW050347160826
845677LV00014B/3843

* 9 7 9 8 3 5 2 0 4 4 8 8 9 *